# Historic Augusta & Augusta College, Kentucky

"It is one of the most beautiful situations on the Ohio."

# Historic Augusta & Augusta College, Kentucky
## SESQUICENTENNIAL 1797-1947

### WALTER RANKINS

COMMONWEALTH BOOK COMPANY
ST. MARTIN, OHIO

Copyright © 1949 by Walter Rankins
Originally published in a limited edition of 250 copies
Copyright © 2023 by Commonwealth Book Company

All rights reserved. No part of this book may be reproduced in any form
or by any means without the prior written consent of the
publisher, excepting brief quotes used in reviews.
Printed in the United States of America.

ISBN: 978-1-948986-64-9

To the memory

of my

Mother and Father,

Emma Taylor and Albert Edwin Rankins

who had a prominent part in the educational and business life

of Augusta.

## Introduction

"Only a farmer or a farmer's son can tell you why some apparently sleepy towns often exert an influence for miles around far exceeding that of larger places.

Augusta, Ky., on the slopes of the majestic Ohio River Valley, 49 miles southeast of Cincinnati, is such a town. The old houses along its shaded streets have peered down on the passing parade of great historic eras in American life, and have sheltered families whose sons have influenced the destinies of whole continents.

Augusta's old houses, stately and simple in style and line, have stood through all the decades since. Within the warm color of their old red brick walls was born and raised a galaxy of outstanding sons and daughters.

Here, too, humbler folk — itinerant preachers, wandering printers, farmers, merchants and families moving from Kentucky — crossed from Augusta to Ohio's fertile regions on Boude's Ferry, just as the autoist can use a more modern version under the same name today.

Augusta has always been one of the most picturesque of the Ohio River towns. From the time when the river served as the great migration route to the Northwest Territory, it has always been a good place to put in for shelter at night, to take on supplies, or to ride out a period of shallow water.

In the community's 150th year the descendants of the settlers who first came from Virginia's Piedmont are fulfilling the aspirations of their pioneer forebears: to live in peace amidst beauty and plenty, in a quiet and gracious corner of the great American continent."

## ACKNOWLEDGEMENT

I wish to thank Miss Marie Dickore' of Cincinnati for permitting me to copy from her article in "Tracks" (a C & O publication) the introduction to this book, and I am most grateful for the records she has furnished from her valuable Americana;

Mrs. Ben Harbeson, Mrs. Crawford Gilkeson, and Miss Georgia Harbeson for the use of their cherished pictures and the facts concerning the Bradford and Marshall families;

Mrs. Alberta Harvie and Mrs. Robert B. Powers for their help and encouragement;

Mrs. Mark Helm of Indianapolis, Indiana for her letter from Mr. Josiah K. Lilly of Stephen Foster's visit to Augusta.

Mr. Will Rankins for relating to me the story told him by Senator Joe Blackburn. Mr. D. B. Cline for his drawing of the town plat from town records. Rev. O. S. Crain for the use of his history of the Methodist Church.

Mr. Marshal Crouch of Cynthiana, Ky. for the Ohio River pictures. Mr. J. W. Crumbaugh for his pen drawing of the Augusta Female College. Mr. John E. Thompson for his technical assistance;

And all those who have helped, as I have sought to gather the scenes and events of the past and to hold them as an unforgettable memory.

Walter Rankins

# CONTENTS

| | Page |
|---|---|
| Situation Acclaimed | 1 |
| Town Charter | 3 |
| Early Town Trustees | 3 |
| Bracken Academy | 4 |
| Augusta College | 8 |
| Stephen Foster Visits Augusta | 21 |
| Augusta Female College | 24 |
| Battle of Augusta | 25 |
| Augusta Male and Female College | 26 |
| Cultural Surroundings | 27 |
| Industrial Period | 29 |
| End | 30 |

## ILLUSTRATIONS

I   "It is one of the most beautiful situations on the Ohio."
II   First Court held in Augusta. Dickinson Morris home
III   A Building of the Bracken Academy, Established in 1798
IV   "Martin Marshall Homestead" — on Riverside Drive
V   The J. B. Ryan Home, one of the early Augusta homes
VI   Original Building, Augusta College, Augusta, Ky.
VII   "Gen. John Payne, Doctor J. J. Bradford Home, on Riverside Drive, the birthplace of Laura Bradford Marshall."
VIII   Ancestral home of General George C. Marshall — Augusta, Ky.
IX   Marshall, Bradford Home on Riverside Drive
X   "Dormitory of the First-Established Methodist College in the World." —Frankfort Street
XI   The College Building on Bracken Street, where Hanson Penn Diltz wrote "Hollow Bracken."
XII   The B. F. Power Home on Elizabeth Street
XIII   Augusta Female College 1852-1860
XIV   Augusta Male and Female College 1868-1896
XV   The Home of William J. Rankins and Jane Silverthorn Rankins
XVI   The F. L. Cleveland Home, on Fourth Street
XVII   The Sylvanus McKibben Home on Williams Street
XVIII   The O'Neill Ferry, across to Boude's Landing, an Early Gateway to the Miami Valley
XIX   The Augusta Public and High School, a Large Gymnasium Has Been Added.
XX   Knoedler Memorial Library
XXI   Within this Row was the Girl's School of Miss "Birdie" Blades
XXII   "Where the River Runs in a Direct Course for Several Miles"

# Historic Augusta and Augusta College

Nestling among a bower of trees on the edge of the Blue Grass region of Kentucky lies the town of Augusta. "It is one of the most beautiful situations on the Ohio," where the river runs in a direct course for several miles and where the sunsets send a riot of color aloft to gold the clouds against the blue of the early evening sky, while the shadows of light and dark silhouette the high Kentucky hills — and as the day closes a blanket of purple and grey envelope the low rolling Ohio hills, that seem to extend down to the very water's edge of the river's bend, to make the setting and the scene one of the most beautiful in all the world.

Founded in pioneer days, Augusta's influence was destined to extend to the remote corners of the earth.

"As early as June 1773, Robert McAfee left his company, who had reached Limestone Creek (Maysville, Ky.) and made an excursion through the contiguous country. Passing up Limestone Creek to its source, he struck across the dividing ridge to the waters of the north fork of Licking, and proceeded down the stream some twenty or twenty-five miles, and then directed his course over the hills of the present county of Bracken, to the Ohio River. When he reached the river, he ascertained that his company had passed down. Determined to follow as speedily as possible, he instantly went to work, and, with the use of his tomahawk and knife, cut down and skinned a tree, and constructed a bark canoe, which he completed about sundown on the same day of his arrival. Committing himself to the frail craft, he floated down the river, and on the succeeding day — the twenty-seventh of June, overtook his company at the mouth of the Licking."[1]

In the year 1775 a party composed of ten men—Samuel Wells, Hayden Wells, Thomas Tebbs, John Tebbs, John Rust, Mathew Rust, Thomas Young, William Tripplett, Richard Masterton, and Johnithan Higgs—came to what is now Bracken County.[2] They stayed only a short time as the Indians were operating out of the Licking River, and the Miami towns were not far distant, making Bracken County untenable. So they turned back to Limestone (Maysville) and Washington to the companionship of other parties who had come down the Ohio and had located there.

These men had found in Bracken County mute evidence of a great struggle between a race of men said to be almost of giant size, traditionally called

---

[1] Collins *History of Kentucky*. Page 453.
[2] Land Book—Mason County Ky.

White Indians (Welch) and the American Red Indians. The Red Indians, by superior numbers, had exterminated their foes, and the site of what was to be Augusta had been probably one of its most decisive battles.

"A letter from General John Payne who has resided many years in Augusta, and who was an active, brave, and efficient officer under Harrison at the Mississinaway towns, and on the north-west frontier during the last war with Great Britain, gives the following interesting account of the ancient remains discovered in that place:

"The bottom on which Augusta is situated is a large burying ground of the ancients. A post hole cannot be dug without turning up human bones. They have been found in great numbers, and of all sizes, every where between the mouths of Bracken and Locust creeks, a distance of about a mile and a half. From the cellar under my dwelling, sixty by seventy feet, one hundred and ten skeletons were taken. I numbered them by the skulls; and there might have been many more, whose skulls had crumbled into dust. The skeletons were of all sizes, from seven feet to the infant. David Kilgour (who was a tall and very large man) passed our village at the time I was excavating my cellar, and we took him down and applied a thigh bone to his—the owner, if well proportioned, must have been some ten or twelve inches taller than Kilgour, and the lower jaw bone would slip on over his, skin and all. Who were they? How come their bones there? Among the Indians there is no tradition that any town was located near here. When I was in the army, I inquired of old Crane, a Wyandott, and of Anderson, a Delaware, both intelligent old chiefs (the former died at Camp Seneca in 1813), and they could give no information in reference to these remains of antiquity. They knew the localities at the mouths of Locust, Turtle, and Bracken creeks, but they knew nothing of any town or village near there. In my garden, Indian arrow heads of flint have been found, and an earthen ware of clay and pounded muscle. Some of the largest trees of the forest were growing over these remains when the land was cleared in 1792."[2]

"On the 19th., day of November 1794, the King of England at his palace, signed the treaty of peace between his country and the United States of America.

"His Majesty will withdraw all his troops and garrisons from all posts and places within the boundary lines agreed by the treaty of peace. This evacuation shall take place on or before the first day of June one thousand

---

[2] Collins *History of Kentucky*. Pages 209-210.

seven hundred and ninety-six . . . All settlers and traders within the precincts of jurisdiction of said posts shall continue to enjoy unmolested all their property . . ."[1]

So the settlers would be unmolested and they could found their settlements "where they will." That was good news.

Captain Philip Buckner had acquired this site, Augusta, for his Revolutionary War service and had laid off the town in lots, streets, and alleys. And in the October 2, issue of the **Kentucky Gazette,** in the year 1795, there is an account of a sale of lots at public auction on the third of November, six months credit for one-half of the purchase money and twelve months for the other half; and Philip Buckner's Augusta lots changed hands.

There came to this part of Mason County many of the most prominent and wealthy families from the towns of Washington and Limestone: thus, Augusta began to grow. They migrated to this promising location, with its fine harbor and its lovely situation, to cast their lot in a new and fast growing part of the county, and were later to become prominent citizens and early trustees of Augusta.

Bracken County became a county on December 14, 1796, and was taken from Mason County.

With the petitions of the men who had purchased lots and had located here, an act was passed by the Kentucky Legislature for establishment of a town by the name of Augusta, and the following men were appointed trustees: Francis Wells, Robert Thome, Robert Davis, James Meranda, John Boude, John Hunt, and Joseph Logan.

On October 2, 1797, at the request of Philip Buckner, these trustees met with him and negotiated for the six hundred acres of land on which Augusta is located.

John Hunt and William Hord went the security of the trustees in the amount of one thousand pounds, and a record was to be made with the court.

The second meeting of the trustees was not held until the fifth day of June, 1798, at the home of Robert Davis; the next meeting at the home of Thomas Broshiers in June 1798, when Vachel Weldon was duly elected a trustee.

The following men were early trustees: Nathaniel Patterson, David Starks, Charles McClain, Dickinson Morris, William Buckner, Thomas Broshiers, Robert

---

[1] *Kentucky Gazette*, August 1, 1795.

Schoolfield, Philip Ebert, John Sells, James Armstrong, John Marshal, James Donovan, John Payne, Dr. George W. Mackie, Abraham Patterson, Robert Smith, John Schoolfield, Thomas Nelson, Samuel Thomas, Dr. Anderson Keith, John Blanchard, John E. McCormick, David Davis, Joseph Morris, and Martin Marshall, Esq.

Besides the trustees the buyers of lots were the following: Messrs. Brown and Beel, Isaac Meranda, Goldsmith Case, David Brunnel, John Davis, Samuel and William Brooks.

Not only were these men hardy pioneers but they were men of culture, education and refinement, and there was added to this the finest of Virginia womanhood with their grace and charm: families of Taliaferro, Lee, Keith, Marshall, Doniphan, Barker, Meyers, and Payne.

And on this account, and as well as the favorable location, an act was approved by the Kentucky Legislature, December 22, 1798, as follows:

"That Philip Buckner, Nathaniel Patterson, Samuel Brooks, William Brooks, John Blanchard, Francis Wells, Robert Davis, John Boude, John Fee, John Pattie, and Joseph Logan shall be, and are hereby constituted a body politic and incorporate, and known by the name of the trustees of the Bracken Academy."

Thus the Bracken Academy became a part of Augusta's life.

A very imposing series of buildings was erected at the southeast corner of High and Elizabeth Streets, long the home of Mrs. Bell Meyers. There was the brick building on Elizabeth Street with a series of low wood rooms as a dormitory, fronted by a continuous portico and extending to a large brick two-story building for classrooms, and situated on High Street.

On June 5, 1799, lots were again sold at public auction. Joseph A. Smith was the auctioneer, and the following were buyers: Vachel Weldon, Nathaniel Patterson, Charles McClain, Robert Davis, Philip Buckner, Samuel Brooks, William Brooks, Francis Wells, John Blanchard, Dickerson Morris, who was also the clerk of the sale. These lots, comprising almost the entire town, sold for $2,519.25.

Roads began to be opened out of Augusta. An act was passed opening a road from Georgetown to Augusta. "Whereas it is represented to the general assembly, that the public would be benefited by opening a road from Georgetown to Augusta, in Bracken County.

"Be it enacted by the general assembly, that William Henry and Richard M. Gano, of Scott county, Samuel M'Million, James Caldwell and James Coleman, of Harrison county, and William Woodward and Philip Buckner, of

First Court held in Augusta. Dickinson Morris home

A Building of the Bracken Academy, Established in 1798

"Martin Marshall Homestead" — on Riverside Drive

The J. B. Ryan Home, one of the early Augusta homes

Bracken county, be appointed commissioners, and are hereby vested with full power to cause a wagon road to be opened from Georgetown, through Scott count, Harrison county, and Bracken county, to Augusta, having due regard to the nearest and best way; and should any person, through whose waste land the said road should be viewed, object to the opening of the same, the sheriff of the county in which the land may be, shall, at the direction of the said commissioners, summon a jury to meet upon the land on a certain day in the commissioners' order mentioned, who shall be qualified to ascertain the damages that may arise by the opening said road; and the road shall not be opened until such damages shall be paid by the commissioners.[1]

"Upon motion George W. Mackey to postpone the opening of the streets in the town of Augusta until the first day of November next, upon the proposition of Philip Buckner to obtain the establishing of a road from Ferry Street opposite to High Street to intersect the road to Pendleton, May 1814."

A petition to open a road to Berlin was made in 1822. Augusta, with its roads to the inland towns, with its harbor so well located for an easy access, became a shipping center to all of central Kentucky.

The early commercial life of the town centered around the market house, a commodious building for these early days. It was 20 x 45 feet, the floor paved and the house enclosed.

It was the year 1814 and the laws governing the operations of the market house were of necessity hard and stringent.

Some of them were:

"That from one hour before sunrise until nine o'clock from the first day of December to the first day of March and from half an hour before sunrise until eight o'clock for the balance of the year, on Wednesday and Saturday of each week shall be the time of market.

"That all food except provender for cattle or horses either animal or vegetable shall be considered articles of marketing.

"That no person shall sell or buy any article of marketing within the limits of town of Augusta except at the market house, under penalty of $2.00 if a free person or not less than five or more than 10 lashes for a slave.

"That no person shall sell any article for a higher amount than he paid for it.

"That any free person or owner of a slave may pay the regular fine of a slave, and thereby the penalty of lashes will be revoked."

---
[1] *Littels Laws*, Page 201.

The first water system was installed by John McCormack:

"Order that John E. McCormick permitted to dig a well in the town at the foot of the hill at the end of Main Street, provided said McCormick keeps the same secure and not injure said road, only while digging, permitted to convey the water to his own house by **pipes,** not injuring the street." [July 1819.]

And the first recorded business house was that of David Starks:

"The trustees of Augusta will Please make a deed for the house and part of the lot to David Starks where his hatters shop is and oblige them. Philip Buckner, Oct. 26, 1799."[1]

"Dr. John N. Tomlinson and Dr. Jonathan Bradford," of the long line of the noted physicians in Augusta, 1833, were made the first board of health; and the first private schools were those of Mr. Henderson, who had a boys school in the Town Hall; Richard Keene, a graduate of Trinity College, Doublin, instructor of distinction; and Z. Harmon, an English gentleman, who had a school for boys and girls.

"Bracken Sentinel, Augusta, Kentucky — 9/2/1820

"LITERARY NOTICE

The Subscriber takes this method to inform his friends, that he has opened a

s c h o o l

For the reception of Scholars, in that spacious house of Captain Buckner's, in Augusta.

Terms — Three dollars per quarter, and no extra charges except only for wood.

The first class will particularly attend, every morning to the exemplifications of English Grammar according to the late, easy and much approved method. Therefore, any one whose avocations prevent him from attending all day, can have the privilege of this class during their exercises.

The late improvement received under some of the most distinguished teachers in the United States, induces me to think that I can teach a pupil more in one month now than I used to do in three.

Z. HARMON"

---

[1] Official records of the City of Augusta, Ky.

"N. B. — A few young Ladies or Gentlemen can be accommodated with Board, at or near the School — where they can be forwarded in Geography, with the use of MAPS, and in the most useful Branches of English Literature."

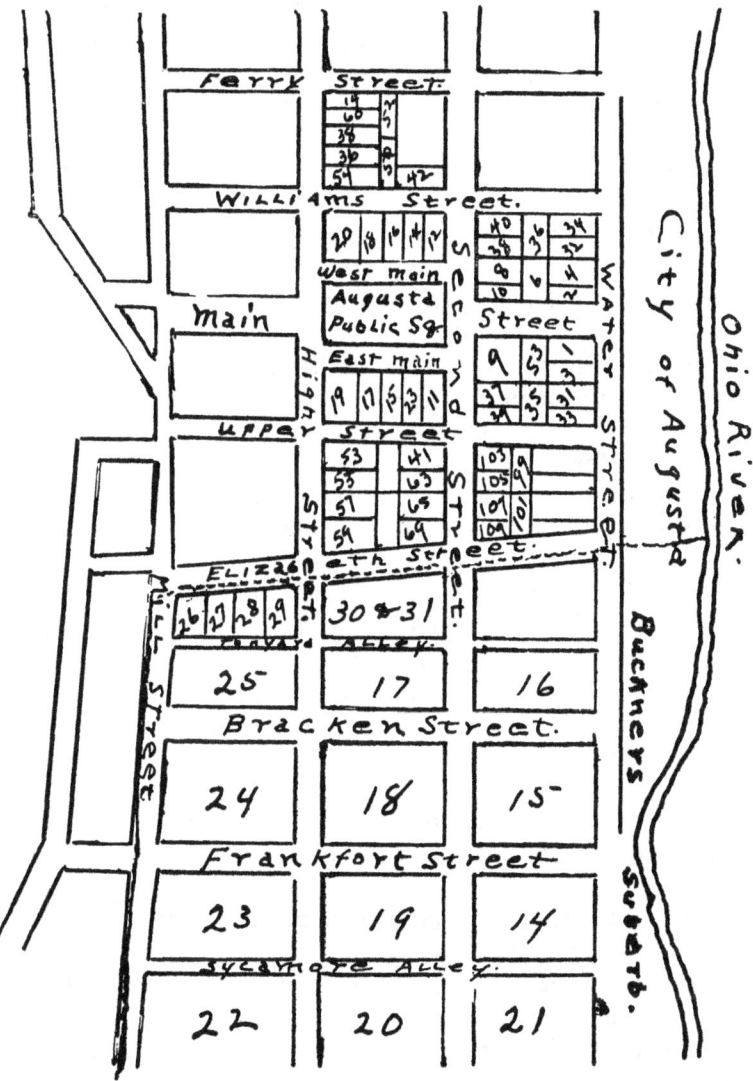

In 1824 William Buckner gave to the town of Augusta all the streets and alleys in Buckner's Suburb for $1.00. These streets and alleys—his property—were Water, Second, High, Mill Streets, Tanyard, Cherry, Vine, Cedar, Sycamore and Seminary Alley's. And a plat was to be made showing the location and numbers of the lots as now constituted the town.

The first ferry, town controlled, was across the Ohio River, in 1822.

Augusta was at one time the county seat of Bracken County, and the county court met in a building located on the Public Square. This building was erected as early or earlier than 1824 and was destroyed by fire on April 20, 1848.

The county seat had been moved to the village of Brooksville, near the center of the county.

The most important and far reaching event in Augusta's early history was the merger by the trustees of the Bracken Academy with conferences of the Methodist Church of Ohio and Kentucky to found the Augusta College. The year was 1822.

"Augusta College, one of the best literary institutions of the west is located here. It is under the patronage of the Methodist Episcopal Church, and was the first college ever established by that denomination in the world."[1]

Cokesbury of Maryland was the first college organized by the Methodist Church but owing to a disastrious fire it was in existence for such a short time that Kentucky historians claimed the first **established** Methodist college was at Augusta.

Dr. George Savage who wrote a history of "Methodist Institutions of Learning in Kentucky", wrote in 1889: "On Dec. 15, 1821 the commissioners of the two Conferences met at Augusta and after consultation with the trustees of Bracken Academy, they jointly determined upon the establishment of the first Methodist College in the world at Augusta, Bracken County, Kentucky, under the title of Augusta College."

Dr. Daniel Stevenson, a president of the Augusta Male and Female College and a professor at Centre, in an extensive survey found it to be true that the Augusta College was the first established Methodist college in the world.

Thus the foundation of the great educational system of the Methodist Church owes its beginning to Augusta.

The campus occupied several acres beginning at High Street and extending to Water Street, where there was its largest dormitory, and extending over Bracken and Frankfort Streets. The College buildings were supplemented

---

[1] Collins *History of Kentucky*, Page 210.

ORIGINAL BUILDING
Augusta College, Augusta, Ky.
The First Established College in Methodism. Commissioners appointed 1820.
Chartered by Legislature of Kentucky, December 7, 1822.
Building erected 1825.   Building destroyed by fire 1856.

"Gen. John Payne, Doctor J. J. Bradford Home, on Riverside Drive, the birthplace of Laura Bradford Marshall."

by other buildings in the town.

There were students from many states. They came by stagecoach, horseback, steamboat, and probably ox cart, which was a common means of travel.

"Among other things, the Conference of 1823 was busy with a report from the trustees of Augusta College and the work of organizing it as a college was in the near future. Eleven delegates to the ensuing General Conference were elected and among them was Peter Cartwright.* It was he who was, also, associated with the founding of three institutions of learning in Illinois: McKendree College, Illinois Wesleyan College and the University of Illinois."**

The aims and purposes of the College are set forth in an advertisement in the Cynthiana Observer, October 15, 1825, of a new newspaper of the Augusta College:

"This Journal is to be edited by the President and Professor of Augusta College, in Kentucky, and is to be under the especial patronage of the Methodist Episcopal Conferences in this State, and in Ohio. Its objects are of the highest importance in the interests of literature, science, politics, morals and religion. Its income is destined to the support of the rising seminary, whose trustees must belong to the class of Christians already named.

"Though our College is destined to advance the cause of a united literary and religious education among our own people, and to raise the standard of our ecclesiastical as well as our social character, yet we aim at making not only good Methodist Scholars and Christians, but to contribute in making good Scholars and Christians for every department and class of society. Our institution emphatically is not to be sectarian, but is earnestly desirous of harmonizing with all the other institutions of the State and the West."

Other revenue was derived from the Augusta Herald and the ferry rights in the town, — its greatest investment source of income.

Colleges were rare in the midwest in the year 1820, and as a new adventure required the best thought and talent, careful consideration was given to the selection of the first officers and teachers of the Augusta College.

Rev. John P. Findley of Ohio had been appointed to the Kentucky Conference to found the preparatory department. He was the son of Rev. Robert Findley, educated at Princeton, "and as the main building had been erected through the munificence of Capt. James Armstrong, a layman of the Methodist

---

\* Doctor Geo. Savage, 1889, Methodism in Kentucky by W. E. Arnold.
\*\* Dr. John Owens Gross, *Christian Advocate*, February 20, 1936. Page 87.

Church, with the aid of a few friends, the preparatory department was fully organized by August 1824, when Captain Armstrong died."[1] but he had lived to see the fulfilment of what must have been a great desire accomplished.

John P. Findley died in May 1825 and his remains rest in the rear of the old Methodist Church on Riverside Drive in Augusta, where have resounded the voices of so many eloquent ministers.

The Collegiate Department was organized in the year 1825 and Martin Ruter, D.D., of Massachusetts, "known as the foremost Methodist educational leader of his day",[2] was made the first president. He was afterwards president of Alleghany College and founded the first Methodist college in Texas, which is now Southwestern University.

To be under the guidance and instruction of this exceptional man was ample reason of these pioneer boys to travel such long distances, under severe hardships, and for some of them to leave their homes so young in life, at the age of twelve. It was this background of courage and determination, and a vision of so resplendent a future that has made America great.

Joseph S. Tomlinson, A.M., who was pronounced by some "the ablest debater in America"[3] followed Martin Ruter as president and continued as president until the College charter was revoked. He was then offered the presidency of Ohio University but declined and became a member of the faculty. His brother was Dr. John Tomlinson, the physician of Augusta, and they were brothers of Eliza (Tomlinson) Foster, wife of William Foster, the parents of Stephen Collins Foster, the writer of so many lovely American folk songs.

Some of the faculty members were:

Henry Bascom, the great Methodist preacher, later a bishop of the Methodist church, Chaplain of the United States House of Representatives, and President of Transylvania College.

John P. Durbin, writer and traveller, who was later to become the President of Dickinson College, Pennsylvania, and Chaplain of the Senate of the United States.

Herman Johnson, President of Dickinson College during the Civil War;

Frederick A. Davis, M.D., Professor of Chemistry and Botany; Ira Root; Thomas H. Lynch, later a member of the faculty of Transylvania; John Vincent; Dr. Caldwell; E. W. Gray; Professors Robbins; Harrison; W. H. Stewart; Hon. Frank L. Cleveland, the father of Justice Harland Cleveland of Cincinnati;

---

[1] Methodism in Kentucky by W. E. Arnold. Page 63.
[2] Ibid
[3] Ibid

Rev. Burn H. McCowan, D.D.; Rev. Dr. Simpson, D.D.; and Mr. McLeod, instructor in Elocution.

Among the trustees were John Chambers, Governor of the Iowa Territory; Rev. Joshua Soule, a bishop of the Methodist church;

Martin Marshall, Esq., a widely-known Kentucky lawyer and a cousin of Chief Justice John Marshall. It was in his office that many boys studied law. He was the son of Rev. William Marshall of Mason County, Kentucky. Martin Marshall's son, William Champe Marshall, was educated at the Augusta College, studied law in his father's office, was a state representative for several terms and a trustee of the Bracken Female Academy. He was the father of George Marshall who fought as a boy in defense of his home town, Augusta, during the Civil War. He became an important industrialist in Pennsylvania.

George Marshall married Laura Bradford of the talented Bradford family. She was the daughter of Dr. Jonathan J. Bradford of Augusta, a noted Civil War doctor, and the sister of Dr. Thomas Stuart Bradford, a prominent Augusta physician, a graduate of Jefferson Medical College.

George and Laura Bradford Marshall had four children: William C., born in Augusta, who died when a small boy; Stuart, who was born at Samuel Euwing's estate, "Meadowland" in Pennsylvania and graduated from Virginia Military Institute; Marie, born in Augusta and married Dr. Singer, and George Catlett, born at Uniontown, Pennsylvania, a short time after the family left Augusta.

He was in Augusta when a small boy and again at the age of seventeen, just before entering Virginia Military Institute, and visited the home of his uncle's family, Dr. Thomas S. Bradford and his wife, Margaret Marshall Bradford.

George Catlett Marshall was later to thrill the world with his military genius, was Chief of Staff of the United States Army, and was sent to China on a vitally important mission of settlement affecting the enire world, and has held so successfully, in one of the most critical periods of American history, the most important diplomatic position in our government, the Secretary of State of the United States.

Other wealthy and important men who were trustees were: John Armstrong, Maysville; Rev. George C. Light, Frankfort;

Gen. John Payne, Esq., who entertained William Henry Harrison at his home on Riverside Drive;

Arthur Thome, Esq., Augusta; George Doniphan, Esq., Augusta; Squire G. Shopshire of Augusta; Gideon Minor, Esq., Clermont County, Ohio; Rev.

James Savage, Germantown, Kentucky; Samuel Lewis, Esq., Cincinnati, Ohio;

Reverend O. M. Spencer, Cincinnati, Ohio, a Methodist minister who served in the Ohio Militia, president of the American Bible Society, a famous writer, and a civic and religious leader in the Cincinnati region;

Rev. John Meek, West Union, Ohio; Francis Landrum, Augusta; John Todd, Esq., Augusta; Dr. George W. Mackie, Augusta; Alfred Powell, Esq., Augusta; Marshall Key, Esq., Washington, Ky.; and Rev. Peter Acies, Louisville, Kentucky.[1]

With a faculty of such eminence and trustees of wealth and influence it was only natural that the student body of the College should be recruited from the most prominent families of Methodists in the United States, and that others should seek this college for the education of their sons. And this accounts for the number of graduates and students who added to the intellectual life and progress of these early days.

Numbered among its alumni were: Dr. Randolph Sinks Foster, son of Isreal and Polly Kain Foster, who became the president of Northwestern University, later, pastor of St. Paul's Church, New York City and the second president of Drew Theological Seminary; Dr. John W. Miley, a member of the faculty of Drew Theological Seminary; John Gregg Fee, who championed the anti-slavery cause and who founded Berea College;

William S. Groesbeck, internationally-known financier of Cincinnati;

Gen. Durbin Ward, born in Augusta, a Union officer who lost an arm at Chicamaugua and for his gallantry won a high honor, a United States District Attorney and in the Ohio legislature;

Dr. William H. Taylor, in the College at its closing and graduated from Ohio Wesleyan and from Jefferson Medical College who, with Dr. T. T. Bradford, assisted the famous Kentucky surgeon, Dr. Joshua T. Bradford, of Augusta, in his skilled surgery;

Benjamin F. Power, who helped to establish the tobacco markets in Cincinnati, then the second largest in the world and who was active in making Augusta a leader in the prizing and shipping of tobacco which was the wealth of so many prominent August families. The leaders were James A. Powers, F. L. Powers, P. B. Powers, B. S. Rankins, R. P. Hamilton, T. S. Hamilton, William Allen, T. H. Armstrong, James W Jennings, C E. Robertson, Thomas Weldon, Reynolds Hook, and J. D. McKibben.

Other prominent alumni were:

Joseph Longworth of Cincinnati, whose grandson, Nicholas Longworth,

---

[1] Catalogue of Augusta College — 1829.

Ancestral home of General George C. Marshall — Augusta, Ky.

was Speaker of the United States House of Representatives, and whose granddaughter is Clara Longworth, the Countess de Chambrun;

Thomas H. Whetstone of Cincinnati, who was the first president of the Union Literary Society;

William P. F. Hulbert, a successful real estate and business man of Cincinnati whose grandson, Hubert Taft, is one of Cincinnati's most prominent men. Wiliam Hulbert's daughter married Peter R. Taft, a brother of President William Howard Taft;

William H. Wadsworth of Maysville, Kentucky, a lawyer and member of the Congress of the United States;

Thorton F. Marshall of Augusta, a lawyer of distinction and in the Senate of Kentucky. Though a Democrat, he cast the deciding vote that kept Kentucky in the Union;

John A. Boude of Augusta, a well-known lawyer and judge;

J. B. Clark of Brooksville, Kentucky, a lawyer and United States Congressman;

Dr. Phillip B. Gatch of Ohio, the son of the noted pioneer Methodist preacher, Rev. Philip Gatch;

General Alexander William Doniphan, born in Mason County, Kentucky; graduated Augusta College in 1826 with great distinction, particularly in the Classics; read law in Hon. Martin Marshall's office; member of the peace conference (1861) Washington, D. C.; member of Missouri legislature several terms, and a hero of the Mexican War.

Major John W. Breathitt, Hopkinsville, Kentucky, a prominent lawyer and county judge and a nephew of Governor John Breathitt of Kentucky;

Silas Field of Missouri, a brother of Judge Emmett Field of Louisville, Kentucky, whose father, Larkin Field, was an eminent lawyer. His cousin, Curtis Field of Richmond, Kentucky, also was an alumnus. These men were descendants of a brother of the progenitor of the famous Field family of Stephen Field of the Supreme Court of the United States and Cyrus Field who laid the Atlantic Cable;

Judge Joseph Doniphan, who studied law in Martin Marshall's office; in the legislature of Kentucky and a circuit judge.

Dr. Louis Marshall, M.D., brother of Chief Justice John Marshall; A.M. degree from Augusta College, Minister of the Methodist Episcopal Church in Virginia, first president of Hillsboro, Ohio Female College, and president of Washington College, now Washington & Lee University.

James Armstrong, a merchant and philanthropist, whose grandson,

Stuart Walker, born in Augusta, organized the Stuart Walker Players of Cincinnati, Indianapolis and Hollywood, of histrionic fame;

Milton E. and Austin M. Clark, brothers, of Brown County, Ohio, originators of the Clark and Gruber Mint at Denver, Colorado;

The Hall brothers; Calvin D., Alfred J., William C. and Thomas J., Jr., of Pendleton County who joined the Confederate Army;

William Paxton, a lawyer, who studied law in Martin Marshall's office and was the author of "The Marshall Family".

In the roster of the Union and Jefferson Literary Societies will, no doubt, be found many noted men.

## UNION LITERARY SOCIETY—

B. F. Anknevy, Illinois; William Adair, Tuscumbia, Alabama; J. S. Allbreck; W. W. Anderson, Augusta;

Prince Bennett, Michigan; Karl H. Brooks; J. E. Broadureal of Cynthiana, Ky.; F. C. Brooks, Michigan; Foster H. Blades, Shelby City, Kentucky; J. H. Banks, New York City; L. H. Berry, Newport, Kentucky; J. H. Brown, Brownsville, Virginia; J. C. Bland, Vicksburg, Mississippi; Joseph Black, Ohio; E. Bettas, New Carthage, La.; D. DuBose, Richardson, Louisiana; William Buckner, Georgetown, Ohio; Duval Payne Boude, Augusta; John W. Breathitt, Hopkinsville, Kentucky; Granville Barrere, New Market, Highland County, Ohio; Judge John Boude, Augusta; John Bonton, Brownsville, Virginia; Sam C. Curren, Claysville, Kentucky; M. B. Cotton; F. L. Cleveland, Augusta, Kentucky;

A. M. Clark, Brown County, Ohio; M. E. Clark, Brown County, Ohio; G. P. Clark, Augusta; J. B. Collins, Texas; J. W. Cotton, Memphis, Tenn.; J. T. Cochrain, Vicksburg, Mississippi; George Cassiday, Zanesville, Ohio; Samuel Carson, Shelby County, Kentucky; Thomas R. Colson, Rushville, Ohio; William A. Collard, Augusta; L. A. W. Cheafant, Felicity, Ohio; A. B. Cook, Vicksburg, Mississippi; David Chiles, Minerva, Kentucky; W. H. Cougill, Clark County, Maine; Dr. Ruben H. Carnal, Alexandria, Louisiana; J. B. Cotton, Alexandria, Louisiana; William Dacey, Indiana; M. F. Damarat, Portsmouth, Ohio; Abraham Diltz, Augusta; G. F. Duke, Kenescha Salines, Virginia; W. A. Doniphan, Augusta;

Henry Edmondson, Scott County, Kentucky; J. W. Ellington, Greenup City, Kentucky; W. R. Elliott, Franklin, Louisiana; William H. Edwards, Liberty Hall, Kentucky; James B. Fetstone, Mayslick, Kentucky; R. Folkes, Vicksburg, Mississippi; Curtis Field, Richmond, Kentucky; O. H. Field, Missouri; Silas H. Field, Missouri; Benjamin F. Fox, Natchez, Mississippi; George Grafton, Pine

Ridge, Mississippi; William S. Gordy, Louisiana; A. Geddard, Kentucky; E. P. Gains, Warrenton, Mississippi; O. Griffin, Cincinnati; Henry V. Gispan, Augusta; G. W. Groves, Carthage, Louisiana; William Gibbons, Augusta, Kentucky; William S. Gum, Vicksburg, Mississippi;

W. A. Harris, La Grange, Tennessee; Thomas Howell, Augusta; Edward Howell, Maine; Elijah Howell; Jas. Humphrey, Port Gibson, Mississippi; E. A. Hamilton, Augusta; Dana Hubs, Laurenceburg, Indiana; E. James, Louisiana; Francis Jordon, Pennsylvania; John R. Keith, Augusta; F. D. King, New York, N. Y.; F. E. King, New York, N. Y.; F. P. King, New York; I. W. King; John H. Locke, Louisville, Kentucky; E. M. Lane, Vicksburg, Mississippi; I. Locke, Louisville, Kentucky; Henry Lackie, Alexandria, Louisiana; H. M. Lnney, Harrodsburg, Kentucky; Henry Lackie, Alexandria, Louisiana, G. W. Leinn, Baltimore, Maryland;

Alfred Murry, Bracken County, Kentucky; Alfred I. N. Myers, Augusta; M. C. Martin, Alexandria, Louisiana; W. M. Matthews, Natchez, Mississippi; Thomas H. Whetstone, Cincinnati, Ohio; W. H. Mackie, Augusta; Thomas Morton, Mason County, Kentucky; William McDowell, Portsmouth, Ohio; Josiah M. McKay, Portsmouth, Ohio; H. Moore, Pittsburg, Mississippi; John McConthy, Trimble City, Kentucky; John Muing, Bracken County, Kentucky; W. D. Williams, Clarksburg, Virginia; William C. Miller, Millersburg, Kentucky; James McNeal, Grand Gulf, Louisiana; George Marshall, Augusta, Kentucky; C. W. Murphy;

James L. Nash, Louisiana; W. Nottingham, Florida; F. Nash, Attakapas, Louisiana; G. M. Nash, Jefferson City, Mississippi; John W. Ovny, Baltimore, Maryland; Will W. Orr, Augusta; William D. Penyton, Selamena City, Tennessee; W. R. Pierce, Poplar Plains, Kentucky; A. Bruce Porter, Kentucky; J. L. Pogeke, Naucarthaga, Louisiana; W. C. Purer, New Carthage, Louisiana; Elijah C. Phister, Maysville, Kentucky; B. W. Payne, Augusta; Thomas Powers, Augusta; L. Price, Lexington, Kentucky; B. F. Power, Augusta;

John H. Quinn, Hillsbourgh, Ohio; O. P. Raynolds, Kentucky; Samuel H. Rehy, Washington, S. C.; William Russel, Wilmington, Ohio; E. W. Robertson, Plaqueman, Louisiana; D. L. Ryan, Mercer City, Kentucky; Walter Ring, Augusta, Kentucky; William J. Rankins, Augusta, Kentucky; Jom B. Ranels, Franklin, Louisiana;

Henry A. Shaefer, Port Gibson, Mississippi; John Stockwell, Kentucky; Milton C. Smith, Mason City, Kentucky; W. M. Soule, Lebanon, Ohio; Steven P. Shaifer, Port Clinton, Mississippi; E. W. Smith, New Carthage, Louisiana; John K. Smith, Attakahas, Louisiana; Dr. C. S. Savage, M.D., Bracken County,

Kentucky; S. H. Sisson, Augusta, Kentucky; F. M. Sell; C. O. Scott, Alexandria, Louisiana; William Salter; Richard A. Stone, Warren, Mississippi; Johnithan Short, Kentucky;

Benjamin . Taylor, Augusta; L. P. Thomas, Augusta; John G. Tomlinson, Augusta; C. C. Tomlinson, Harrodsburg, Kentucky; W. C. Tomlinson, Augusta, Kentucky; Dr. W. H. Taylor, Augusta; David Thomas, Augusta, Kentucky; Osuet H. Vick, Vicksburg, Mississippi; A. Vandorn, Port Gibson, Mississippi; William Watson, Hazen, Mason County, Kentucky; William D. Williams, Clarksburg, Virginia; W. H. Wadsworth, Maysville, Kentucky; W. T. Walker, Fleming County, Kentucky; Thomas J. Wilson, West Feliciana, Louisiana.

## JEFFERSON LITERARY SOCIETY — Partial List

Ransom Brooks, Cincinnati, Ohio; John Bradshaw, Shelbyville, Kentucky; Arron Biddison; W. R. Brown; G. Brading; Fredrick P. Clay, Frankfort, Kentucky; William Campbell, Cynthiana, Kentucky; James R. Clark, Brown County, Ohio; Stephen Cobb, West Feliciana, Louisiana; John W. Casaett; Thomas Dobyns, Mason County, Kentucky; Joseph L. David, Butler County, Ohio; William Dowsing, Columbus, Mississippi; Charles Dyas; Daniel Evans; L. S. Espy; Jeremiah H. Foster; D. Florey; William S. Groesbeck, Cincinnati, Ohio; S. S. Gray; Prof. E. W. Gray; Jesse Garlinghouse, Augusta; S. P. Hall; G. M. Hardwick, Tuscaloosa, Louisiana; John Hieght; W. E. Hinze; William F. Jones; Philip Kennedy; Josiah Lamborn; Robert Loving, Nelson County, Virginia; Wm. B. Lakin; Jessie Lock; Edward Love; Stephen Lock; W. T. Leener; S. L. Leanord; Alex Mcyntire; A. L. C. Magruder, Jefferson County, Mississippi; Samuel Melvin, Accomec County, Virginia; H. McCasland; B. F. Morris;

Doctor A. H. Pollock, M.D., Bracken County, Kentucky; David Portes; Addison Reese, Cynthiana, Kentucky; John Rees, Georgetown, Ohio; John Rossell; George W. Robinson; J. W. Ricks; Augustus W. Ruter, Augusta, Kentucky; Paul Riggs; Alexander D. Spencer, Cincinnati, Ohio; Thomas Simpson, Adams County, Ohio; W. H. Stewart, Brown County, Ohio; Samuel C. Spencer, Cincinnati, Ohio; (Thos. Jefferson Nicholas Simmons); J. Snider; W. L. S. Simmons; I. R. Starkey; P. S. Spawling; William G. Starky; L. F. Vandene; Stephen Wood, Adams County, Mississippi; Isaac Newton Williams; William R. White and Henry C. Whitney.

## OTHER STUDENTS — Partial List

Robert Aldredge, Tuscumbia, Alabama; James Armstrong, Augusta; Richard H. Anderson, Green County, Kentucky; Edward L. Anderson, Green County,

Marshall, Bradford Home on Riverside Drive

"Dormitory of the First-Established Methodist College in the World."
Frankfort Street

Kentucky; Joseph H. Anderson, Vicksburg, Mississippi; William J. Anderson, Vicksburg, Mississippi; William Bailie; J. H. Bishop; A. Bascom; I. S. A. Bradshaw; R. R. Bailie, Baker; Kit Best, Bracken County, Kentucky; D. H. Bishop; Nelson Berrere, New Market, Highland County, Ohio; Spencer J. Ball, Mason County, Kentucky; William I. T. Buckner, Augusta, Kentucky; John T. Bate, Jefferson County, Kentucky; Erasmus D. Beach, Hamilton, Ohio; Thomas Carter, Clinton, Louisiana; Charles Cabell; John L. Carey, Bridgenville, Delaware; Joseph Chambers, Washington, Mason County, Kentucky; Joshua A. Clark, Hayswood County, Tennessee; William P. Cook, Warren County, Kentucky; L. A. Clinton, Louisiana; Granville L. Cookrill, Tuscumbia, Louisiana; Wallers S. Chew, West Feliciana, Louisiana; Philemon L. Chew, West Feliciana, Louisiana; George H. R. Clark, St. Louis, Missouri; John Cochran, Brown County, Ohio; Alexander C. Crawford, Philadelphia, Pennsylvania;

Adam C. Deem; I. C. Damron; Robert V. Davis, West Feliciana, Louisiana; Robert B. Ellis, Todd County, Kentucky; Collins Elliott, Butler County, Ohio; Fredrick Farrer, Washington, Mississippi; Thomas P. Farrer, Washington, Mississippi; Asa Foster, Bourbon County, Kentucky; Orvil Grant; Abner Green, Jefferson County, Mississippi; W. P. Grayson; William W. N. Gibson, Warren County, Mississippi; H. S. Garland; Davis S. Goodloe, Tuscumbia, Alabama; Henry E. Gill, Mason County, Kentucky; Gorden R. Gilmore, Cincinnati, Ohio; George J. Griffin, Hinds County, Mississippi; John S. Griffin, Jefferson County, Kentucky;

George H. Harrison, Warren County, Ohio; Thomas L. Haile, St. Francisville, Louisiana; Matthew Hopple, Cincinnati, Ohio; James B. Hinde, Urbana, Ohio; Augustus F. Holton, Augusta, Kentucky; William P. F. Hulbert, Cincinnati, Ohio; William P. Hamilton; J. W. Harmon, Augusta, Kentucky; J. B. Jackson; William Jones; Charles A. Jones, Cincinnati, Ohio; William Johnson, Humpsted County, Arkansas Territory; Moses H. Keener, Ridgeville, Ohio; Charles R. Kincheloe, Nelson County, Kentucky; Rodney King, Adams County, Mississippi; Richard E. King, Adams County, Mississippi; William B. Lewis, St. Landry, Louisiana; James Leigh, Perquumans County, North Carolina; Edward Lawrence, Cincinnati, Ohio; Preston Lodwick, Cincinnati, Ohio; John Long, St. Francesville, Louisiana; George Long, St. Francesville, Louisiana; G. W. Leinn, Baltimore, Maryland;

Sidney H. Monroe, Falmouth, Kentucky; Nicholas B .T. Marshall, Augusta, Kentucky; Thomas N. Marshall, Augusta, Kentucky; William B. Magrufer, Fluvanna County, Virginia; Hilleary Magruder, Fluvanna County, Virginia; Thomas G. McIntyre, Franklin County, Mississippi; William S. Meek, Tuscaloosa, Alabama; Thomas W. Miller, Scioto County, Ohio; Daniel B. Nailer, Vicksburg, Mississippi; Stephen E. Nash, Monroe County, Mississippi; Samuel Nixon, Lowdon County, Virginia; John H. Oglesby, Madison, Indiana; George W. Dutten, Augusta, Kentucky; John W. Peryman; Charles M. Phillips, Baltimore, Maryland; William Preston, Louisville, Kentucky; Henry B. Price, Washington, Mississippi; Charles M. Phillips, Baltimore, Maryland; J. C. Richey; Augustus Robbins, Augusta, Kentucky; Sam'l Rossell;

Henry L. Rucker, Augusta, Kentucky; Pascal F. Right, Amelia County, Virginia; Stephen S. Rossel, Washington City; William H. Robertson, Mason County, Kentucky; John Rees, Georgetown, Ohio; Charles Rabb, Natchez, Mississippi; Luke Robinson, Cambridge, Maryland; Phelander S. Ruter, Augusta, Kentucky; James Ryan; Chancy B. Shepherd, Matthews County, Virginia; Samuel R. Shakleford, Amite County, Mississippi; William B. Smith, Cincinnati, Ohio; Joseph W. Sessions, Adams County, Mississippi; Joseph J. B. Southall, Murfreesboro, North Carolina; Samuel H. Smith, Cincinnati, Ohio; Henry Smith, St. Louis, Missouri; Samuel A. Spencer, Cincinnati, Ohio; Francis W. Spencer, Cincinnati, Ohio; Lucien D. Stockton, Flemingsburg, Kentucky;

William Schoolfield, Augusta, Kentucky; Baldwin H. Spiker, Winchester, Tennessee; Caleb L. Swayze, St. Landry, Louisiana; David M. Stiles, Claibourn County, Mississippi; William M. Stiles, Claibaurn County, Mississippi; Glenn G. Stoudemire, Louisville, Alabama; Joseph P. Sanford, Baltimore, Maryland; William B. Smith, Cincinnati, Ohio; James A. Thome, Augusta, Kentucky; John H. Thomas, Wilkinson County, Mississippi; Charles W. Thorp, Cincinnati, Ohio; James L. Thorp, Cincinnati, Ohio; George Tribbey, Augusta, Kentucky; John Vincent;

Richard A. Whetstone, Cincinnati, Ohio; Benjjamin Whiteman, Green County, Ohio; Stephen T. Wood, Adams County, Mississippi; Peter G. Winn, Claysville, Kentucky; William Wayland, Batavia, Ohio; George R. Waters, Bracken County, Kentucky; William Watts, Maysville, Kentucky; Alexander H. Whitney, Jefferson County, Mississippi; Silas Woods, Lebanon, Ohio; Charles W. Walden, Cincinnati, Ohio.[1]

The college papers of the literary societies were: The Jefferson Chronicle, Friday Courier, and The Evening Herald.

These men gave special lectures to the Literary Societies:

Rev. Dr. Tefft; Judge McLean; Dr. Thompson; Rev. W. I. Fee of Ohio; Dr. McCullom, who often "appeared in the hall" and was always "invited into the room" to give an interesting biological lecture.

---

[1] Minutes of the Union and Jefferson Literary Socities.

The College Building on Bracken Street, where Hanson Penn Diltz wrote "Hollow Bracken."

March 23rd 1832—Jefferson Society:

"Motion was then made to appoint five to meet a committee from the Union Society to request the Hon. Henry Clay to address the two societies on the next commencement."

The records show that the faculty of the College, including Dr. Ruter, were honorary members of the societies and took part in the debates.

In the societies quills were used for pens and fat was preferred to oil in lamps.

"The days of College prosperity were the days of Augusta's renoun and greatest prosperity.

"It was a center on which all eyes from all parts of North and South, East and West looked with an interest; for there were congregated some of the great lights of the church as scholars, divines and orators, and they were going out, the educated sons of the church, to make their impress upon society in after years."*

The homes and the hearts of this cultured little town were opened to the students, and the gayety of many social events in these lovely old homes can be visualized. The college building on Bracken Street, with its colonial stairway, its large stately rooms, no doubt, was the scene of many brilliant social events. Yet the seriousness and close comradeship that abounds in colleges of this type (for it was typical of the early English schools) are apparent from this one incident of a Cincinnati boy.

"Meeting Extrordinary June 9th., 1831"

"By order of the President the Society met in order to consult what would be the most suitable manner of manifesting their sorrow and regret for the demise of one of their honored and respected members Mr. Ramson Brooks, one whose social virtues, moral conduct, and accomplished talents entitle his memory to be perpetuated in the hearts of his fellow members and deeply impressed on their fondest recollections. After the president had stated the object of the meeting the following resolution was introduced by Mr. Portis and immediately adopted by the House: 'Resolved unanimously, that the members of the Jeff. Society, in commemoration of their departed friend and fellow member R. Brooks, wear crape on their left arms for thirty days.' Mr. Rozel was appointed to inform by letter, the Rev. Brooks of the proceedings of this society

---
* J. W. Cunningham — Newport, Kentucky, 1869.

with respect to his son. Mr. Melvin was selected by the House to purchase and distribute the crape necessary for each member. There being no other business the House was adjourned.

"Sam'l Smith, President
"W. H. Stewart, Secretary"

Strict discipline was required, in these early days, and the right of free speech was seemingly denied — as witnessed in the following trial of Josiah Lamborn:

"August 5th 1829—Jefferson Society

The Society met persuant to adjournment—the role being called, the Prosecutor of the Society arraigned before the members, Josiah Lamborn for certain offences against the dignity of the Society contained in the following prosecution. (viz)

Jefferson Society
Augusta College

Whereas it hath been represented to us by certain individuals, belonging to this Jefferson Society, that Josiah Lamborn, a member of the said Society, hath wilfully and without any regard for the dignity of this Society, expressed himself in a manner degrading to the standing and contrary to the laws laid down in the constitution of said Society.

Therefore I Thos P Haille, by the powers invested in me, as Prosecutor in behalf of the Society aforesaid and agreeable to the Constitution in such cases made and provided do hereby arraign before the members of this Society the said Josiah Lamborn to answer to the charges preferred against him in this Endictment

Witness Thos G. McIntyre President of the Jefferson Society, the 5th day of August Eighteen hundred and twenty nine.

Thos P Haille Prosecutor

After which the Society submitted to a hearing of the trial Thos P. Haille Pros. and Addison Rees in behalf of the Society—A. O. Spencer and Ransom Brooks for Deft — Several witnesses being examined and the counsel on each side having finished pleading, The Society decided the offender (on refusing to make acknowledgements) should be suspended from all privilges of the Society for the Term of one month from the commencement of the next session.

The Society then appointed a Committee to inform the Faculty that it would submit to any arrangement the Faculy might think proper to make with respect to marching at the Commencement, after which the Society adjourned

**Alfred H Pollock Secty."**

The B. F. Power Home on Elizabeth Street.

1852 - 1860

There is no record to show that Josiah Lamborn ever made acknowledgement of this accusation but the records do show that he was taken back into the full fellowship of the Society and was appointed to make the next 4th of July address.

Augusta College conferred the honorary degree of L. L. D. on George Robertson, Chief Justice of Kentucky and one of Kentucky's most honored men.

High on the hill back of Augusta, there was a very old negro church. The darkies sang early and continued until late, and their musical, harmonious voices floated softly over the quiet of the town. Stephen Foster came often to visit his uncles, Dr. Joseph Tomlinson who was president of the College and Dr. John Tomlinson, the physician. He was in Augusta with his mother in 1833, at the age of seven years, an impressionable age, and it can hardly be doubted that he heard many of these songs in their happier vein and was impressed by them. He was to put into song at a later time the sorrow that their voices reflected.

The Tomlinson family was zealously anti-slavery and intensely interested in this controversial question. With the College, it was then a moral and not a political issue. Dr. Tomlinson was to lead Augusta into the Northern Conference, the only one in the Circuit to leave the Southern Conference.

So, the slavery question must have been often discussed in the Tomlinson homes and, as there was a daily packet from Cincinnati where Stephen Foster was living at the time, it would **hardly** be an **exaggeration** to infer that he often visited the families of his prominent relatives and heard much of the plight of the darkies of whom he was later to create a folklore of songs beloved by all of the world.

Henrietta Foster, sister of Stephen, also, was in Augusta. She was afterwards the grandmother of Henrietta Crossman, the actress, who was to make the character of "Rosalind" live in the hearts of the American people.

The slavery question had long been a vital one among the student-body, but at first this and related questions, though often discussed, resolved themselves into but one decision: that slavery should be abolished by governmental decree.

They seemed to realize that the question was so important that it might bring about a dissolution of the government.

The records show clearly this interest and concern. As early as November 7, 1828 the subject for debate was: "Would it be policy in the United States to abolish slavery?" Decision in the affirmative.

"Is involuntary slavery justifiable in any case?" Decided in the negative. Dec. 9, 1831.

"Should the United States pass a law to prohibit the extension of slavery?" Nov. 8, 1848. Decided in the affirmative.

"Do the signs of our times portend a dissolution of our political union?" Nov. 8, 1848. Decision in affirmative.

"Would it be to the interest of the citizens of Kentucky to abolish slavery?" April 21, 1848. Decision in affirmative.

"Would it be good policy in the citizens of Kentucky to abolish slavery?" July 14, 1848. Decided in the affirmative.

The first signs of disagreement came with the withdrawal of some of the faculty to take a leading part in Transylvania College in 1842.

Henry Bascom of Augusta College who joined the pro-slavery cause was Transylvania's first president under the Methodist regime.

Dr. Daniel Stevenson graduated from Transylvania under the presidency of Dr. Bascom. He was elected Superintendent of Public Instruction of Kentucky on the same ticket that elected Abraham Lincoln president. He reestablished Union College of Barbourville, Kentucky, and was one of the founders of Kentucky Wesleyan and President of the reestablished Augusta College.

"Undoubtedly one of the most decisive contributions to christian education in Kentucky during the last half of the Nineteenth Century was Dr. Daniel Stevenson."*

The Ohio Conference continued until later, but its support was withdrawn with the establishment of Ohio Wesleyan College at Delaware in 1842.

The College continued under the Kentucky Conferences until 1846 when the Northern Conference of Kentucky became its sole sponsor.

Dissension among the students even yet can be noticed. The following record gives a clue to rising feelings:

"June 26, 1846

"Gen.

"We are sorry to find that the majority of the members of the Jefferson Literary Society have little

---

*Dr. John Owen Gross, Pres., Union College.

magnanimity and we regret that we are again compelled to call upon the trustees of the Baptist Church for the use of said church.

"Respect'y yours,
"R. G. Stirling Sct.
"Union Literary Society."

In the minutes of the Jefferson Literary Society, dated June, 1849, the heading is: "UNDER THE NEW ADMINISTRATION," and the closing, is P. S. "STRONG TALK OF LEAVING, COLERA, FEVER, RAGING, ETC., ETC." And August 24: "RESOLVED that the Secretary be instructed to call a public meeting of the Jefferson Literary Society for the purpose of making some disposition of the property of the Society at as early a time as possible in some public journal."

"B. F. Morris"

"The Augusta College trustees having sold to Sarah Armstrong and mortgaged to John Armstrong the ferry rights in the town of Augusta from the Kentucky to the Ohio shore and a resale was made to (Dr.) Joshua T. Bradford, and as the Legislature at the last session repealed the charter of the Augusta College, it is recommended that a law be passed giving title to the Ferry rights to Joshua T. Bradford."

"To many, paradoxically, the greatest glory of Augusta College was in its ending. It was the center of the anti-slavery movement in Kentucky, and the feeling against the College became so intense that the legislature repealed its charter."* And this may account for the sentiment that was directed against Augusta in the Civil War that was to follow.

And so came to a close an institution so well-founded and with the prospect of so glorious a future. It had lived only twenty-seven years, but in those years it had lived vitally and with a high purpose, and that accounts for the number of men who were attracted to it, who loomed large in the life of America.

Dotting the cities of the United States and the remote corners of the earth are the Wesleyans, institutions of learning, moral culture, and progress, and they had their beginning in the Augusta College.

Surely the influence begun in this small town has extended to the far corners of the earth.

---

* Dr. Gross, Union College.

The Bracken Female Academy was chartered by the legislature in 1836 and occupied the former Bracken Academy buildings. Misses Louise and Julia Prinz, from Virginia, were the first teachers, and Henry Bascom was one of its first trustees.

Mr. and Mrs. Thomas S. Orr established the Augusta Female College in the Augusta College building, and among the teachers were Miss Eliza McCracken and Miss Jane Silverthorn, of Virginia; the latter became the wife of William J. Rankins.

The building was damaged by fire in 1852 and burned in 1856 and a new and more modern one was erected. Mr. Orr had died and Mr. A. C. Armstrong had married Mrs. Orr, and the Augusta Female College was continued. Mrs. Mary Armstrong Lauderbach, who founded the D.A.R. Chapter in Bracken County was their daughter.

Samuel Wass built the first part of the cobblestone grade from Main to Upper Street for a contract price of $1,000; the trustees gave his wife and children an additional $500, and J. Wiggerman and Company completed almost the entire grade at a contract price of over $6,000, making the total cost approximately $8,000. It was an exceptionally fine piece of work, and as Charles Dickens said of the Cincinnati levee, " . . . hardly a blade of grass could be seen." A road down to the low water mark was of the same construction, but was covered with gravel. The time was 1845 to 1849.

John Taylor operated a treadmill ferry across the Ohio River. Run by horses, it was probably an advanced mode of operation for a small town.

The compromise of 1859 proposed by Henry Clay had quieted to some extent the slavery question. The appearance of Mrs. Harriett Beecher Stowe's **Uncle Tom's Cabin** in 1852 had provoked bitterness between the North and the South.

Mrs. Harriet Beecher Stowe was a daughter of Lyman Beecher, a noted preacher of Cincinnati. She had a girls school in Cincinnati, and Marshall Key's daughter was a pupil. He was a trustee of the Augusta College. On a visit to Kentucky, Harriet Beecher stopped at the home of Marshall Key in Washington, Kentucky, and saw a sale of negroes at the auction block at the old court house. It is said that she, there, received her inspiration for her book.

Civil War was being carried on between the states. Augusta seemed to be in a very vulnerable position as letters of concern were sent to the Augusta trustees by Maysville, Ripley, and Felicity, Ohio, offering aid. It is significant that the mayor and city council (F. L. Cleveland, S. T. Powers, Dr. J. J. Bradford, W. S. McKibben, T. F. Marshall, B. H. Rankins, and Joseph Doni-

1868 - 1896

The Home of William J. Rankins and Jane Silverthorn Rankins

The F. L. Cleveland Home, on Fourth Street

The Sylvanus McKibben Home on Williams Street.

phan, mayor) appropriated $1,500 for 100 stand of arms, April 25, 1861, and made it unlawful to sell any gunpowder. The home guard had been organized of nonpartisan men to guard against marauding bands.

The attack at Augusta seemed to be a surprise attack.

"At the headquarters of the U.S. Forces, at Maysville, Lieut. Col. H. Blair Wilson, Forty-ninth Ohio Infantry, received about dusk on the evening of the 27th of September a special messenger. He brought intelligence from Ripley [Ohio] that Colonel Basil W. Duke, with about 750 of John Hunt Morgan's men and two small pieces of artillery, had attacked Colonel Bradford's command at Augusta, just 16 miles below Maysville, and after a most desperate resistance on the part of Colonel Bradford and his men, succeeded in capturing Colonel Bradford's entire force.

"The fighting had been desperate, and the toll was tragic. Killed and wounded among the Union to 12 or 15. The loss of the Confederates was estimated to be between 75 or 100 killed and wounded, among them 8 or 10 officers. Among the Confederate losses George D. Prentice, of Louisville, wounded mortally, and a Lieutenant Wilson. The Conferedates left some of the dead and wounded on the field. These were cared for by Augusta men and women. The raiders took horses, buggies, wagons, and all means of available transportation necessitated to carry off their dead and wounded.

"Among the Union disabled and killed were Dr. W. H. Taylor, N. B. Worthington, John B. Story, George Byers, Oliver Stairs, John Gephart, John Perkins, W. Gregg, and Alpheus McKibben. The prisoners were all taken from town as rapidly as they could march. Some of them were later paroled and returned home.

"Much of Augusta was destroyed, the loss estimated [September 28] at $100,000. The principal sufferers were Thomas Meyers, J. B. Ryan, W. D. Dietz, W. P. Taylor, Mrs. Howk, T. F. Marshall, V. Weldon, J. T. McKibben, and Mrs. Barr.

"We hope these cruel outrages upon the people of this state are unavoidable. We hope it may fully appear to be so; but if the Tenth Kentucky Cavalry, raised around Augusta and this place [Maysville] had been left to defend them it could not have chanced."[2]

Augusta's progress had been retarded but not its schools.

Prof. B. T. Bluett continued the Augusta College and Prof. G. M. Yancy established the Augusta Male and Female College.

---
[1] Letter to H. G. Wright from Joseph Doniphan, mayor of Augusta—J. W. Crumbaugh.
[2] Letter to H. G. Wright ORU & C.A.A.P.C. et Series 1 Vol XVI p. p. 1011 ff.

From the Bracken Chronicle August 24, 1871:

## AUGUSTA
## *MALE AND FEMALE COLLEGE*

The next Session of this Institution will begin on the 11th day of September, 1871.

A full corps of Teachers is secured to take charge of the different Departments.

The course of study is such as is found in the best schools and colleges (male and female.)

For further particulars address,

G. M. YANCEY, A. M.

There were private schools also. Professor Bricket, of Harvard University, conducted a select girls' school in the second floor rooms of the home of Mr. James Kinney. Mr. Richard Mitchell had a school in the home afterwards owned by Mr. and Mrs. Kendall Morgan.

Mr. Mitchell married Miss Belle Rankin. Later he was head of the Augusta College, and after his death Mrs. Mitchell continued the College; later she married Hon. F. L. Cleveland.

Dr. Daniel Stevenson in 1879 reorganized the Augusta College, a co-educational school, and it again had the support of the Methodist Conference. It continued until 1887 when it was acquired by the town trustees and became a public and high school.

Augusta has had fine hotels. They have been well appointed and have entertained many notable people.

The Bodman and Smith hotels were located on Riverside Drive, and colorful Senator Joe Blackburn was a frequent visitor. The story is told of a visit to his suite of a Democratic politician who took a boy from a Republican family to see him, and, with his characteristic good humor, he sent back to this family the story of the man who crawled into a hollow log to spend the night and it rained so hard that the log shrank leaving but a small opening—so small that the man could not get out. He thought of all the mean things he had done, and he remembered that he had at one time voted the Republican ticket, and he felt so little about it that he was able to crawl out this tiny opening.

Congressman Sam Pugh was an important Republican guest and had many torch light parades in his honor.

The Parkview hotel built by T. E. Milner followed these hotels and is an asset to the city.

Bryant's showboat, a leader among showboats on the Ohio, gave its first performance at Augusta, and the John Robinson Circus often showed in the town, to the edification and delight of the small boys.

Augusta was a good Chautauqua town and demanded excellent talent. Among its many attractions were: lectures by William Jennings Bryan and Vice President, Thomas A. Marshall.

Russell Hall, dedicated by Sol Smith Russell, was Bracken County's and Augusta's largest entertainment building.

Augusta became an exceptional community of accomplished and cultured families who, though not provincial, built their lives around their lovely churches and beautiful homes, and this was due in part to the noble heritage of the Augusta College.

These were the families of Taylor, Stevenson, Powers, Marshall, Bradford, Harbeson, Dunbar, Gibbons, Boude, Hamilton, Knoedler, Reese, Steen, Rankins, Norris, Wilson, Armstrong, McKibben, Power, Wittmeier, Clark, Gray, Patterson, Cleveland, Neider, Reynolds, Allen, Ryan Winters, Fulkerson, Weldon, Walker, Toleman, Robbins, Caden, Meyers, Faber, Diltz, Wood, Hobday, Ludwig, Harris, Asbury, Robertson, Bayless, Blackerby, Hook and many others.

The generations that were to follow inherited the spirit and influence of their forebears, and have become prominent statesmen, doctors, lawyers, journalists, playwrites, pharmacists, dentists, educational leaders, newspapermen, high ranking army officers, business men, musicians, and have taken their part in world affairs.

The many fine schools that followed the Augusta College also played their part in this development.

These Schools had given an outstanding opportunity for education to the men and women of Bracken and the surrounding counties, and the culture and the wealth of the many diversified business interests of Augusta were due in part to their influence.

The heads of these business and civic enterprises were: William Gibbons, J. B. Ryan, William J. Rankins, J. Pike Powers, Charles McCormick, Thomas J. Taylor, T. D. Ryan, J. B. Ryan, S. T. Powers, H. C. Liter, Robert Liter, W. W. Orr, Henry Sisson, J. S. Orr, Al Hurm, G. J. Daum, Lewis Weimer, John Fleming, John Armer, S. D. Keen, John Malkus, C. Stevalter, John Bradley, Frank C. McKibben, John Insko, George H. McKibben, George Kerans, H. B. Asbury, M. W. Hagen, Major John Robbins, Henry Bertram, B. F. Ginn, J. E. Dunbar,

B. F. Taylor, J. W. McKibben, W. O. Holmes, P. B. Powers, S. W. McKibben, Clarence Hunter, Mrs. S. D. Crumbaugh, Mrs. Mattie Russell, L. P. Brockman, John Owens, G. W. Edington, Charles Hook, John O'Neill, C. A. Reese, Len Wittmeier, John I. Winter, William McKibben, Sr., J. W. Robbins, James Boude, Charles Federer, Richard Lane, John Burger, William Sayers, F. M. Fulkerson, Frank Barkley, John Kennard, Milton Taylor, R. P. Yates, William Wittmeier, Isaac Reynolds, Dan List, John T. Jackson, William Work, A. D. Pumpelly, Newton Evans, M. T. Flannery, George Given, Charles Bachman, Louis Weber, William Clark, George Teegarden, J. R. Wilson, Frank Bradley, Dr. Charles Rice, James A. Thompson, Edward Thompson, Dr. R. L. Harvie, Dr. Edwin Smith, Dr. Joseph Stoekle, Dr. H. B. Taylor, John Reisser, M. Schweitzer, John Stroube, F. Anderson, Lewis Wolf, Findley Henderson, Louis Jones, Dr. J. E. Robertson, Charles Bradley, James Reese, Edwin Toleman, and others.

Notable among the early business institutions whose influence and trade were far reaching were: The Allen and Harbeson Bank of William Allen, John M. Harbeson and Benjamin Harbeson; The Augusta Milling Company of N. J. Stroube; The G. W. Moneyhon Lumber Co., The John Oldham's Cigar Factory; The John Cablish Bakery; The Farm Machinery business of A. E. Rankins; The L. P. Knoedler and Sons Drug Company of L. P. Knoedler, Phillip Knoedler, Gibbons Knoedler and A. Robbins.

Early professional men were: Master Commissioner J. P. Reese; Judge J. R. Minor; Doctor M. W. Steen, D.D.S.; Joseph Felix Attorney; Judge George Doniphan; Doctor S. D. Laughlin, D.D.S.; Doctor A. A. Mannon, M.D.; Judge Matthew Harbeson, and Doctor J. C. Norris, whose wide experience and medical knowledge made him one of Augusta's most valuable men. And later Attorneys M. Hargett, M. J. Hennessey, and Dr. Charles G. Steen, D.D.S.

The men who followed this generation and those who are continuing these business enterprises and professions are well-known Augusta men and have done and are doing their part to uphold the high standard of their predecessors.

The college building was replaced by the present public and high school system. A large gymnasium has been added.

The list of the professors, teachers and graduates of this school is to be found inscribed in the school archives. It has been a progressive and important Public and High School, with proficient and meritorious professors and teachers and, with the inspiration of the notable schools it follows, it is doing an excellent work in the community.

Augusta was ever mindful that its churches were the bulwark of our

The O'Neill Ferry, across to Boude's Landing, an Early Gateway to the Miami Valley.

The Augusta Public and High School, a Large Gymnasium Has Been Added.

Knoedler Memorial Library

civilization and that they were the most important influence for good. There have been many learned and devout men who were ministers, and great care and pride have been taken in buildings and equipment of its seven churches. They are in order of their founding in Augusta: Presbyterian, Methodist, Baptist, Methodist (Colored), Catholic, Christian and Nazerine.

The Masonic Lodge was the first fraternal organization in Augusta, and others that followed added interest and good will.

Augusta is a city that has kept abreast of the times, and realizing the advent of an industrial period it at once used its energy and time to influence industries to locate here, and they have been of great benefit to the city and surrounding community. The F. A. Neider Company, international in scope; the E. H. Hunnefeldt Company, manufacturing Boss washing machines; the L. V. Marks & Sons Company, with widespread interests that take its product to the large distributing centers; the Kentucky Power Company, a large organization that is statewide. The Augusta Motor Co., whose farm machinery business is extensive. One of the first small cities to have automatic telephones, The Northeastern Telephone Company was organized in Augusta.

**The Reflector** was the newspaper of the college days, and the **Bracken Chronicle** has been owned and published by several generations of the Thompson family, for the city's betterment.

The Knoedler Memorial Library, given by Mr. Philip Knoedler, of Chicago, in memory of his parents, so prominently associated with Augusta, is one of the finest small library buildings of northern Kentucky.

The World Wars have found this community patriotic and loyal. Its sons and daughters have performed their part valiantly and not without bravery and high honor.

Augusta has a Rotary, Lions, American Legion and Veterans of Foreign Wars Clubs and prominent Social Clubs, modern business establishments, and is a city of lovely homes and congenial people.

The Sesquicentennial finds it prosperous and looking "over the years and far away" with a pride in its pioneering fathers and with a hope for a successful and happy future.

A river running 'neath its feet,
An avenue of quiet trees—
A vistaed row of houses old
Withal, a beautiful retreat.


Within this Row was the Girl's School of Miss "Birdie" Blades

"Where the River Runs in a Direct Course for Several Miles"

# GENEALOGICAL CHART

www.ingramcontent.com/pod-product-compliance
Lightning Source LLC
Chambersburg PA
CBHW051808100526
44592CB00016B/2610